"Aggressive Mode Booklet" on Investing - before Diving In.

Understanding the Starting Line of Volatility and Safety Management & their Hefty Intros (and what Modern Computational Investing takes).

<u>1st Edition</u>

by: Samuel Dusciuc

Science major, entrepreneur, investor, and engineering student.

The Contents

The Depth

If you need a diagram to memorize, want to know when to put everything safely away, when to invest in the economy. What critical thoughts on fundamentals you should have with the one caveat of them all (if I had to choose).

What 5 principles to follow no matter what on investing, what 5 principles for making money you should have, what my fundamentals on investing are, books I highly recommend, apps I highly recommend, what websites I highly recommend, and the one final thought I have for new investors? Read this booklet in a day before you start your adventure into investing.

The Description

This booklet is targeted towards teenagers and above regarding financing and investing. Hopefully, dipping your toe here. Will reduce what you didn't know and prepare you for your studies ahead on personal financial goals, management and everything in-between. All the best to all.

May you be blessed.

About the Writing Author

Samuel Dusciuc at 18 years of age worked in construction during the economic collapse of 2008. He then went on to college while working at Circuit City during the Holiday season as the company went bankrupt. Then, earning a B.Sc. in S at PSU during the Summers he worked as staff on the manufacturing floor of an orthopedic manufacturing plant (Thortex) where his father was / is senior programming engineer. He then went on to engineering in computer science at GT and an entrepreneurship in co-founding a biotechnology company by the name of Teleogene LLC. - now known as 2strand Inc.

Purposefully left blank

"An investment in
knowledge pays the best
interest." - Benjamin
Franklin

Update & Down to the Gates of Heaven and Hell

Do you ever feel like everyone tells you about investing to – make sure your portfolio is diversified. But what does that even mean? And more importantly, how and where does one do this? In this book I try to break it down how I do so. Not everyone has the same style or the same mindset. But what all have are the same tools. This booklet's sole purpose is to assist you and those you share this book with (please do pass it along!) on how to do just that. The next page has a diagram.

This diagram is core to the *investment template strategy* style I have set here. It's meant to start you off on the right foot.

Volatility | Wealth | Safety
Management

Preserve Wealth – check every year.

1) Gold, Guns & Food.

2) Savings Account.

3) Federal & State Treasury.

Bonds and CDs from banks.

4) Federal & State Bonds.

5) Precious Metals.

6) Defensive stocks (textile businesses / ancient).

Capital – check every 6 months.

7) Real estate.

8) Money Market Funds (backed by mutual funds in same company only).

9) Mutual Funds Bonds (tax free – retirement).

10) Leading Global Stocks.

Growth – check every 3 months.

11) Growth Stocks.

12) Growth Options.

Speculation – every weekend.

13) Penny Stocks.

14) Swinging Cents (not suggested).

(Categorial Ladder of Investing.)

When to put everything into the "Preserve wealth box."

1) Economy corrects usually every 8 years.

2) What you'll see is leading NASDAQ companies trading at 4 to 6 times what they're making (current examples, Nvidia, Amazon, and Tesla).

3) The thing leading the new bubble (in this case, electronic currencies – bitcoin) stops depressing the value of precious metals – specifically gold.

4) Experts blow off questions from the media about speculating on the leading trend for said bubble. Worry at this point. Start to move funds bellow green line into

above the green line (and defensive stocks if you think you can squeeze the last out of the economy).

5) Small public companies with novel products on the OTC stop growing. Entering NASDAQ is nonexistent. Everyone is watching the bubble at this point. We're in late harvest season of the economy. Markets are making record profits.

6) Pharmaceutical and biotechnology companies on the OTC have an average volume under 200,000 shares. In other words, nobody is investing in scientific discovery and exploration.

7) Companies on NASDAQ report down earnings in clusters from each sector. But as a whole, everything looks amazing.

8) Companies that lead the bubble 8 years ago are faltering and are mentioned in the news trying to invent new products and service briefly by the media. But they fail or have half futile success. Quarterly earnings, kind of suck (examples in the current bubble, Chipotle, Potash Corp., Apple, and Samsung).

9) NASDAQ index has a month with more selling than buying (i.e. red month). A fair imminent sign of a collapse of the economy.

10) Corporate companies are caught in bed with the Government in a wheel like cycle. It's clearly affecting the public (example in the current economy, prescription opioids are considered a nationwide epidemic).

Overall, by **point 4** you should be out and above the green line. By **point 6** you should have sold your real estate property that you wanted to sell.

And by **point 8** you should be well placed in

the ***preserve wealth category.*** Sitting and watching where to get the best deal on market correction.

Note, if you anticipate the market to be fairly harsh (2008 < harsh). Then only hold a couple of your defensive stocks. This is good logic in general as you'll have more capital to invest back into the market.

When to move back into the Economy

1) Take money being generated from the money market funds and put a down payment on the cheap real estate in a developed country (think Airbnb if the real estate prices never go up – you still have something generating income!).

2) See what laws were passed that allow for innovation and new services (i.e. search for the next big companies). If unsure and the waters are too muddy. Look at investing forums and news articles about business activity from institutions like MIT and Oxford. Who's making the top 10 most innovative company of the month list?

3) See what nonprofit companies gave way to for-

profit companies. This will help bring step 2 into view further.

4) See what stocks from your mutual fund stocks start to show a green week, and then a second green week. If you don't have a mutual fund stock. Invest $100 through Acrons or Wealthfront and Vanguard to see where they put the money. Or just call your broker and see what they're doing. By law, they have to give you this information whether you're invested with them or not (i.e. hold an account with them all!).

5) Compare this to the growth stocks before the correction. See if they're still around (statistically speaking, 6 out of 8 should be bankrupt....). This should give you an even better perspective of which companies will be the foundation of the next bubble, and who will be the leaders.

6) Invest in NASDAQ, SP500, and global large market Indexes. Should you suck at all the steps in this section? You will succeed here. Unless the end of the world is why the market corrected.

7) Look at the speculation category. Put no more than $10K there on companies that appear to align with these steps.

Critical Thoughts on Fundamentals

Final thoughts, admittedly, you should be able to spot what will probably be the growth stocks of the NASDAQ in the future bubble. During the current bubble. Companies in the marijuana sector for example – are pressing legislative and social norms, hard.

However, ensuring to follow the steps above and holding off on investing. Gives you financial safety and peace of mind. In other words, move out of all categories fully when the current market bubble is about to correct below the red line (with the exception of defensive stocks you're exceptionally confident in – no more than 3).

The Caveat

If, however? Selling all shares of a growth stock gives you less peace of mind in either the NASDAQ or OTC. Hold onto that ticker if you're willing to lose it all. On NASDAQ, GWPH and Tesla come to mind.

On the OTC, 'TRTC' and 'SFOR' come to thought.

Keep in mind, it would be financially unwise to hold if it's a significant amount that you're not-utterly-and-totally-willing-and-can-afford-to-lose. Sell shares till you find a happy medium of the mind.

The 5 Principles to Follow no Matter What on Investing

1) No matter how lucrative a stock may get? It shouldn't equal more than 15% of all your capital in your portfolio (i.e. exclude retirement percent!).

2) No matter how positive you are about stocks on the OTC. Never put more than 10% of your funds into speculation that is reserved for investing (again, exclude percent set aside for retirement investing). The goal is not to gamble here and to have peace of mind.

3) For all types of stocks (mutual, indexes, growth), follow the *120 – minus your age*. The percent you get is how much capital from your earnings should go into investing. Then from this percent. Take the 10 percent set aside for the

OTC. Don't exceed $20K. Ever, for the OTC. Have a separate broker account for this *speculation investing capital.*

4) About 20% of stocks should be overseas (if playing it safe) and about 50% if you're playing it hard and risky.

5) For all types of retirement ventures (mutual, indexes, bonds, etc.). Follow the *Age – 20* to acquire the percent to save from your capital earned for retirement investing.

A special note:

What percent goes into market investing and what percent of your capital for retirement should be a total of 35% out of your money earned every year. About 22.5% should go into investing with about 12.5% going into retirement.

When you reach your 40's these percent should be equal. These numbers should be flipped at the age of 59.

Overall a special rule of thumb in investing because it's critical regardless to one's goals overall!

The 5 Principles for Growth Stock Investing (or how to make money).

1) Never put the money you're not willing to entirely be able to afford to lose.

2) Never put more than 5K in a growth OTC and more than 10K in a growth NASDAQ.

3) Set a price when you will sell half your shares (up or down). And when you will evaluate the stock again on when to sell half again (up or down).

Note: For the OTC. If you sold half because it was down? Keep the other half there and just let it sit. Not worth taking a loss or fussing over. Leave the investment alone and stop watching it. Move on.

4) Never invest in a stock that doesn't already have a product or service. Ideally, it has multiple services and products.

5) The management must be on LinkedIn or other work-related networking sites (i.e. reputable).

Don't ever underestimate the importance of networking.

My fundamentals of Investing

How to Invest and Where:

The first thing you need to know is that a broker is who handles your purchasing into a company. Same as an accountant at a bank handles your money for your savings. TD Ameritrade is the example of a broker company that is one of the largest in the world. However, some banks want in on the action and many have broker divisions with accountants that are also qualified as brokers.

Myself personally? I like to keep them separate. I don't want a broker to know what my bank statements are and I don't want a bank accountant knowing what my broker account holds in earnings from an investment. I personally went with TD Ameritrade.

They're simply the largest and thus have many company connections. I don't know of any company that I wanted to invest into that I didn't find on their platform (you get what you pay for).

The second option and is relatively new is investing via your smartphone. There is a broker called, "Robinhood:"

https://www.robinhood.com/

Which has broken serious ground in this area. A great way to invest and most importantly. It's free because they're trying to draw in people. So, no fee to buy or sell shares. However, because they're new they don't have every company from every corner of the world. This is just a great way to take a couple thousand. Throw it into Intel. Push notification comes your stocks went up say, 5%. Sell all the shares and then buy into say,

Nvidia.

Repeat.

More stable than gambling and more predictable. It's fun and easy. A quick way to make a couple thousand and as one of my buddies in medical school has done (every morning he buys and sells before starting the day).

Lastly, and worth a mention is the wealthy generally speaking hire a broker to manage their investments or at least consult with from companies like TD Ameritrade. Many companies have even popped up that do this for a very small fee for average income earning individuals.

For example, an app called Acorns? The broker does everything (takes your money and invests it without consultation depending on the amount you give them):

https://www.acorns.com

I put in about $400. So far so good. Steady gains on, "aggressive mode." Just a great cheap way to save

money without thinking
about it to get one's feet wet.

Okay now that we've got the platforms out of the way let's talk jargon:

Shares: This is how a company divides its company up into pieces for someone to invest in their company. The more shares you own? The more of the company you in all manner of speaking will own the company. Hence why the term is coined the company went public - anyone can own a piece of it! I forget how much of a percentage you have to own before you actually are given a seat on the board of running the company but it does happen for wealthy successful investors (Warren Buffet to give an obvious example).

The CON about getting into the company via shares is that if a company is struggling? They just print more shares (so to speak). So last month say John was bragging that he owns 10% of small tech. company and the next month they go from 2 million shares to 1 billion. I've seen it happen.

Suddenly the weight of those shares John owns isn't very much if the price goes up or down.

The last CON (and this is the worst). Is what's called a "Reverse Split." This is where a company starts doing well financially and they say hey, "let's cut away at the outstanding shares" (i.e. how many shares the company has put out for purchase by investors).

So, to give an example. Say John sees a company with a PPS (price per share of .0006 cents). He sees the company has 1 billion in outstanding shares but he notices they no longer have debt and they have 3 pretty good products. So, he buys 200,000 shares.

About 2 weeks later the company announces a reverse split of 2 to 1. John doesn't read the announcement because he forgets to enable push notifications on his phone (you really don't want it to come to this...).

The reverse split is now implemented and John owns only 100,000 shares. Also, the price per share has almost dropped by 20% because of this news and many investors are angry, not buying or selling out of spite after waiting so long for the company to finally be successful. But the company doesn't really care because now big firms and the rich will come to buy a now very successful looking company. You are the one who has lost in this transaction.

John is stuck or what is better called, "getting trapped."

For more jargon and definitions see here if there's a term you don't understand:

http://www.investopedia.com

Researching the World:

This is the hardest part and where people get lazy. They just see a company on the news or in the paper and they see the PPS (price per share) go up and they just buy. At the minimum read every morning for about 30 minutes on what's going on in the world.

If one wants to do this legitimately. You also have to go into the bowels of the Internet, so to speak (in order of importance to me):

1) http://investorshub.advfn.com

2) https://upticknewswire.com

3) https://investorshangout.com/

4) http://otcshortreport.com

5) http://www.siliconinvestor.com/home.aspx

These links and the websites with the apps I have on my smartphone that I have built up (see below the list) is how I keep track of the world's economic movements and search if a company is worth the risk.

My vetting process is as follows:

1) Legitimate founder (no shady background and from a previous large company as a manager, etc.). I watch interviews they give on "upticknewswire.com" or I find them on 'YouTube.' I study their mannerisms; gauge what they're feeling. I look them up on LinkedIn. Seriously, have no shame here. Often, future investors will email and ask questions or concerns they have. See if they're hiring or not is also an extremely good cue.

2) A product. If there's no product and only promises I wait and watch. NEVER invest if there's no product. Period. Promises don't bring revenue.

3) Debt. If there's some debt I'm fine with it but if there's a lot of toxic debt (i.e. debt from loans taken out of emergency with high interest)?

I run the other way. *Fast.*

Don't even bother researching into points 1 or 2. Just forget about it. The company will go bankrupt in all likelihood. Especially if outstanding shares is at 750 million or more. If you see these two things?

Look no further into them.

4) If a company has made it to point number four. There's good reason to get excited.

Here, I look for word on the street on forums such as on the first link. What are people saying on forums such as that? Is it the stock in the most talked about top 10 (the forums have settings where you can sort stocks by most talked about, most viewed, etc.).

Are they bashing the company (there will always be people trying to scare you into selling or buying)?

Are people sharing links, news, and sourced opinions? Excited? What's the "feel"?

All companies ride on greed and excitement. Forums are where you find the gold grit in the muck.

In short, how does the company stack up against everyone else and what are people saying?

Assessment:

Okay, you've now gotten passed all the points above in say the past 24 hours and everyone have made you feel good about this company. Now. Why do you believe you should invest in this company?

Is there a lawsuit they're about to win?

Are they about to partner with a large company on a project on the products they have going?

Are there 5-star reviews on their products on Amazon, Walmart, Newegg - etc.?

Did you buy some of the products yourself and actually try them out?

On the SEC, is debt ratio relative to revenue decreasing?

I have done/checked all the above at one point in time. And was deeply concerned if I saw otherwise.

In other words, if you cannot answer at least some of the questions above?

Do-NOT-INVEST-IN-THE-COMPANY. PERIOD.

Notice, I haven't even mentioned looking at the charts. All the charts reflect is the PPS (price per share factoring everything I stated above). Greed. Emotions. Facts. And everything in between.

It's the roller coaster after you've driven to and purchased the ticket to the amusement park.

Before we go there here is your one and only truth and law in this business:

www.sec.gov

Here you can view the quarter after quarter financials of the company (i.e. they on average release all their financial data to the public 4 times a year). Investopedia.com is once again the place to go if you want to discern what the difference is between say "profit", "revenue", and "capital:"

http://www.investopedia.com

Okay, now not only does the company "look like" a good investment from your research. It also to the degree of your studies via assessment it also has a x___ probability of being a good investment.

Now we go to the charts:

This is the best one available from my observation that is free and readily accessible with any browser platform:

https://www.tradingview.com

And ask yourself this question. Does the price reflect an undervalued company relative to your other options? If yes. Buy shares!

Many investors start here and end here on investing. So, no biggie looking here first. The way I look at it is?

The starting line and the finish line are both the same; in that, they're both just a line on the ground (i.e. crossing the line and deciding what to do). If one gets going and does what's in between (i.e. what I stated above)?

You will do just fine.

Critically Important:

Write down in a journal the full name of the company, the ticker symbol, the date, and how many shares you bought and at what PPS. And, WHY you bought the shares.

Conclusion:

Lastly, look for support on this. Other people that are long-term investors that are older than you. People on forums will in courage you but also bash on you, and generally speaking show their greed. It's good to have those who've been there, around you.

If you desire to trade on more of a daily basis. That does require being able to read the charts very well (people do this for a living - it's called being a day trader).

Here are two excellent sources either way. Recommended to at least read the signs in a chart of "total collapse" or "total success" on the first link and on the second to obtain the course's resources.

Mind you, if you've done the things I pointed out above you will have done 99% of the work already (but such free sources are invaluable):

1) Stockcharts.com

http://stockcharts.com/school/doku.php?id=chart_school

2) Coursera.org (Computational Investing by Georgia Tech.):

https://www.coursera.org/learn/computational-investing

Books I Highly Recommend.

Getting Started in Value Investing (*to obtain proper mindset*) by Charles S. Mizrahi (Author).

The Intelligent Investor (*to obtain proper principles*) by Benjamin Graham (Author), Jason Zweig (Author), Warren E. Buffett (Collaborator).

The Flash Boys (*to obtain a perspective of the history of investing*) by Michael Lewis (Author).

Financial Statements: A Step-by-Step Guide to Understanding and Creating Financial Reports (*to understand fundamentally what the financials are doing*) by Thomas R. Ittelson (Author).

Not a Comprehensive List of Apps I use on my smartphone to keep up to date/research (these are just the most critical!).

TD Ameritrade app. Very well-known broker for investing in almost any company you can think of.

PROS:

Has almost any company you'd want to invest into.

Has a money simulator on the app where you can practice investing with fake money.

CONS:

Expensive regarding trading fees. A nightmare of buttons, charts and technical analysis. Robinhood is too cold on this; TD is a red burning sun of numbers...

Seeking Alpha app. Great place to read articles from investors, entrepreneurs and experts in the field.

PROS:

Very informative individuals with some willing to mentor you if they see you don't know much about a sector or company.

CONS:

More, "prestigious" than some other sources so some might belittle, or poo poo your questions as if you're a dumb idiot (can get annoying). The flip side of things I guess for tipping toe with the knowledgeable.

Stockmobi OTC app.
Relatively new in the investors market but showing promise.

PROS:

Shows a ranked list of tickers (i.e. companies) with the most popularity among daily investors.

CONS:

You'll have to go to Bloomberg's app often to find what the company does as tickers/news feed provides often rarely reveals that to get me started.

Investors Hub App. The most prominent and complex forum regarding the investing world.

PROS:

The wild west of the investing world. You can find all the rumors, gossip, and people who've monitored a company from its inception here. Most are willing to give you the information if you ask and some have invested for decades.

CONS:

The whiners (yes, the moderators don't get rid of them), haters (because their company tanked in the same sector as yours) and scammers are here (try to get you to buy or sell shares) - you've been warned.

Robinhood App. The new broker on the block and perhaps most influential in moving the investing sector into a new direction in the late 2010's.

PROS:

No fees to invest in any company (unlike other brokers).

Free to transfer money in and out of your account.

CONS:

The charts have something to be desired (not exactly - "technical" - at all).

Limited companies to invest in (no OTC for example). TD has them harshly beat here in my honest opinion.

Bloomberg App. A myriad of informational news on almost any company on the planet. The Wikipedia of investors news.

PROS:

A great source for a summary of what a company does and figuring out who they are.

CONS:

Can be overwhelming for new investors. Articles out every day.

Comprehensive List of Websites used (in alphabetical order).

Americanbulls.com

Barchart.com

Corporateinformation.com

Financial Times (ft.com)

Finra.org

Investopedia.com

Morningstar.com

OTCmarkets.com

OTCshortreports.com

Research.stlouisfed.org

Sec.gov

Seekingalpha.com

Stockcharts.com

The Wall Street Journal
(wsj.com)

Themorningbrew.com

Tradingview.com

Valueline.com

A Layman's Glossary of Sorts (In order of importance)

Ticker: A company's name abbreviated in a special way when they go public. For example, Ferrari's ticker is "RACE."

10K form: On the SEC this gives you the year-round financials of a company. It is required by the U.S. Government to be filed by a company if they want to be in the publicly listed in the U.S.A.

10Q form: On the SEC this gives you the quarterly financials of a company. It is required by the U.S. Government to be filed by a company if they want to be in the publicly listed in the U.S.A. as well. It is less detailed than a yearly report but is still highly indicative of how a company is doing overall while assessing them.

Stock: A purchase of shares whereby the owner has ownership of the company whereby the said owner can vote and attend investor meetings with the bosses of the company. If an investor owns enough shares and has a credible background in the company's industry? The executive management may request the hiring of the investor to the board of members or other high management positions in the company.

Bond: The lending of your own money to a company as a bank would. An interest rate is set or a variable one on how much is incurred to be owed back to you on top of the loaned sum. There is also a lending period agreed upon and a penalty if you request payment of the loaned money back sooner.

Mutual fund: The collaboration of several companies to put together a ticker with all their names under it. Whereby when you purchase a share of this ticker it's actually the partial purchase into several company shares distributed by percent of shares each put into that ticker by a said company.

Microsoft's ticker is 'MFST' for example if you want to buy shares just from them. A mutual fund ticker containing the largest number of shares in Microsoft is 'VTSMX' whereby you can as well be an owner of Apple Inc., Facebook Inc., Amazon.com Inc. and, Jonson & Johnson (to name the big names under the ticker).

Fraud Indexes. I mean. Cryptocurrencies.

So, this is how I view cryptocurrency:

1) It is not an investment. As it stands it actually wastes energy by having computers run to unlock more coins.

2) While most currency are not backed by gold anymore. They are backed by the debt of the economy of their respective countries. Crypto-currency are backed only by being limited to a certain amount being released into circulation.

3) This commodity has the advantage of allowing easy payment and transfer across country borders where there can be several currencies in war torn or high trade poor places. All other features any currency like the U.S. dollar has.

Summary: In other words, the only thing cryptocurrency brings is ease of use for people that travel or deal at borders. And it offers a gauge or index of the debt of nations. Ever notice that the most entrepreneurial-indebted-nations have the most cryptocurrencies? But to say it is worth $11,000k+ to the dollar? Speaking of the big one. I cannot stand by that. No matter its features.

Now when I was an undergraduate it's not to say it didn't have a *gold rush* feel. It certainly made or broke certain institutions and made some people wealthy. But the risk was there and is there.

Outcome:

It is a large bubble. People love to speculate and it's good right now. It has new features and people are making the profits they want. But that "want" will answer soon to "need" and "principles" of the economies soon that we value (i.e. Constitutions). Once

Government(s) take it seriously, it will tank and adjust to all other currencies. That is close, there are now 900 crypto-currencies.

Conclusion:

On average the U.S. economy corrects or what we call goes through a depression to adjust for new innovations every 8 years. It has been 9 years since the last one. We are due and crypto-currency is leading it. Many companies (Nvidia, Facebook, Tesla, etc.) trade at many times their actual value (profits divided by debt per quarter). So, only put what you are willing to lose to learn the features and be set up to invest when it pops. If fortune 500 companies are the hot air of this bubble. Crypto equals the film.

At this stage however it's best to see what startup companies are being set to lead the next bubble in the OTC stock market.

I see the economy as planting and harvest (to use an

analogy here finally).. We're in late Summer. Marijuana, genomes, and robotic companies are next. And let's not sorely forget the go green initiative in energy. That is very active as well.

**Purposefully left blank. **

A request:

If you've enjoyed this booklet and have gained new insights and fundamentals.

Please, do leave a review on Amazon. If you'd like to contact me or connect?

I can be reached @

https://www.linkedin.com/in/samueldewsick

A large thank you to family and friends for the feedback and support. All this would not be possible without you.

PS: Stick to U.S. stocks while getting your feet wet for at least a year. Over 50% of all stocks are found in the U.S.

Made in United States
Orlando, FL
04 November 2026

90205456R00038